Eli and Mort the Moose are on their next adventure and this time they are learning to snowboard!

Eli and Mort make learning to snowboard fun! In this book, Eli and Mort learn basic snowboarding terms and actions with a positive 1, 2, 3 twist!

Eli and Mort are dedicated to the loves of our lives, Josh, Heath and Will.

Special thanks to Mark "Spike" Eisenman, AASI-RM Examiner, for his snowboarding expertise and guidance, our editor Brenda Himelfarb, and all of the snowboard instructors that teach this wonderful sport to our youth.

* This book is not intended to be a substitute for professional snowboard instruction at your favorite resort.

Created by Elyssa and Ken Nager.
Character Illustrations by Eduardo Paj.

Published by Resort Books Ltd.

Published by

resort
b**ks

www.eliandmort.com

Mort's Snowboard is Goofy.
(Right foot forward)

Tail

Rear Foot Binding

Heal Edge

Front Foot Binding

Toe Edge

Tip/Nose

Tail

Toe Edge

Rear Foot Binding

Eli and Mort's EPIC Adventure

Heal Edge

Front Foot Binding

Tip/Nose

Eli's Snowboard is Regular.
(Left foot forward)

Today Mort and I are going
to learn to snowboard!

1, 2, 3, It's going to Be EPiC!

First we met our awesome snowboard instructor, Remi.

Remi told us how to carry our snowboards
with the bindings facing out.

1, 2, 3, we DiD It!

Safety first. Next, Remi showed us that when you take your snowboard off, it's safe to leave it upside down in the snow. That way, the snowboard couldn't slip, slide

Down the mountain.

Then we learned how
to put on our snowboard.

We slid our snowboard boot
in the binding and tightened
it. Our foot stayed put.

1, 2, 3, WE
ROCKED
It!

Next, Mort and I learned about the edges
of the snowboard. The edges are used for control.

Our toes pointed to the toe edge of the snowboard.
Our heels pointed to the heel edge.

Now that we knew how to use our edges in the snow, Remi said it was time to try walking uphill.

I thought snowboards only went downhill.
So did Mort.
It took us a couple of tries, but...

1, 2, 3, we crushed it!

With our front foot in the binding, we pushed our snowboard along, like a skateboard on the sidewalk.

This was called skating. Mort and I skated our way to the chairlift and up the mountain we went.

When we reached the top of the mountain, it was time to get off of the lift. Mort and I each took a deep breath, stepped on our board, stood up tall, and...

1, 2, 3, we GLIDED it!

Now that we were up the mountain,
we were excited to head down!

I watched as Mort slowly tried to
sideslip down the mountain.

Oops! Mort fell down!
Then, he got right back up again.

1, 2, 3, Mort Did it!

After Mort ripped it up sideslipping,
we used our edge to
traverse ------ across ----- the mountain!

1, 2, 3, we DiD it!

Then Remi taught us
floating leaf which looked
as though we had dropped
a leaf from the air, and
then watched it float back
and forth.

After all of our hard work,
it was time for a hot chocolate break.

I said, "Snowboarding was awesome."
Mort agreed.

We drank our hot chocolate, then
Mort and I were ready to rock the snow again!

But before we got back on our boards,
we threw some snowballs at each other.

Next we learned Garlands. Mort went first!

For Garlands, Mort balanced on his heel edge, traversed across the mountain, and then sideslipped!

Mort did Garlands on his toe edge AND his heel edge. He didn't want to be a "heelside hero," who Mort says is someone who only does tricks on his heel edge.

**NO WAY!
WE WANT TO DO it all!**

We did so well doing Garlands, that
Remi told us we were ready for S-turns!

Yahoo!

It took Mort a few tries to do S-turns.

I said, "Mort, you've got this."
Mort tried really, REALLY
hard and...
1, 2, 3, Mort
TURNED
DOWN THE
Mountain!

When the day was over,
I dreamt of Mort and me
catching huge air.

1, 2, 3,
We were Fast Asleep.

Mort and I learned:

SKATING
Front foot in the binding, back foot pushes you along.

SAFETY
Safety first!

GLIDING
Sliding forward with the front foot in the binding and the back foot resting on the stomp pad.

SIDESLIP
Sliding on one edge down the mountain.

TRAVERSE
Sliding on one edge across the mountain.

FLOATING LEAF
Sliding back and forth on one edge.

GARLANDS
A traverse with a sideslip.

S-TURNS
Turning from edge to edge.

eliaNDmort.com